Connecting Memories - Book 1

An Adult Coloring Book Designed With
Simple Familiar Black-Line Drawings And Sentence Cuing Phrases
- For Cognitive Art Therapy -

Recommended As A Resource For Therapeutic Recreation Departments
And At Home One On One With A Care Taker Or Family Member

27 Single Sided Coloring Pages

The Adult Coloring Book Craze is Here. And now the older adults can join in on the fun and enjoy the benefits too.

Bonnie has created a great activities resource for elders with dementia that can be used individually, on a one on one basis or in a group setting. Simple familiar designs, color cuing and common phrases allow for successful completion. Providing a positive, calm and fun experience.

I highly recommend its use with anyone with cognitive impairment. Every therapeutic recreation department should utilize this amazing resource as they will immediately see the benefits to their elders.

Recommended By: Alexis Chiucarello, Director Of Therapeutic Recreation And Dementia Program Coordinator Long Term Center

---

Illustrator: Bonnie S. MacLachlan
Publisher: Art.Z Illustrations
Griswold, Ct
www.ArtZillustrations.com
Special Thanks To: Alexis Chiucarello

Made In America

ISBN: 978-0-9970237-5-6

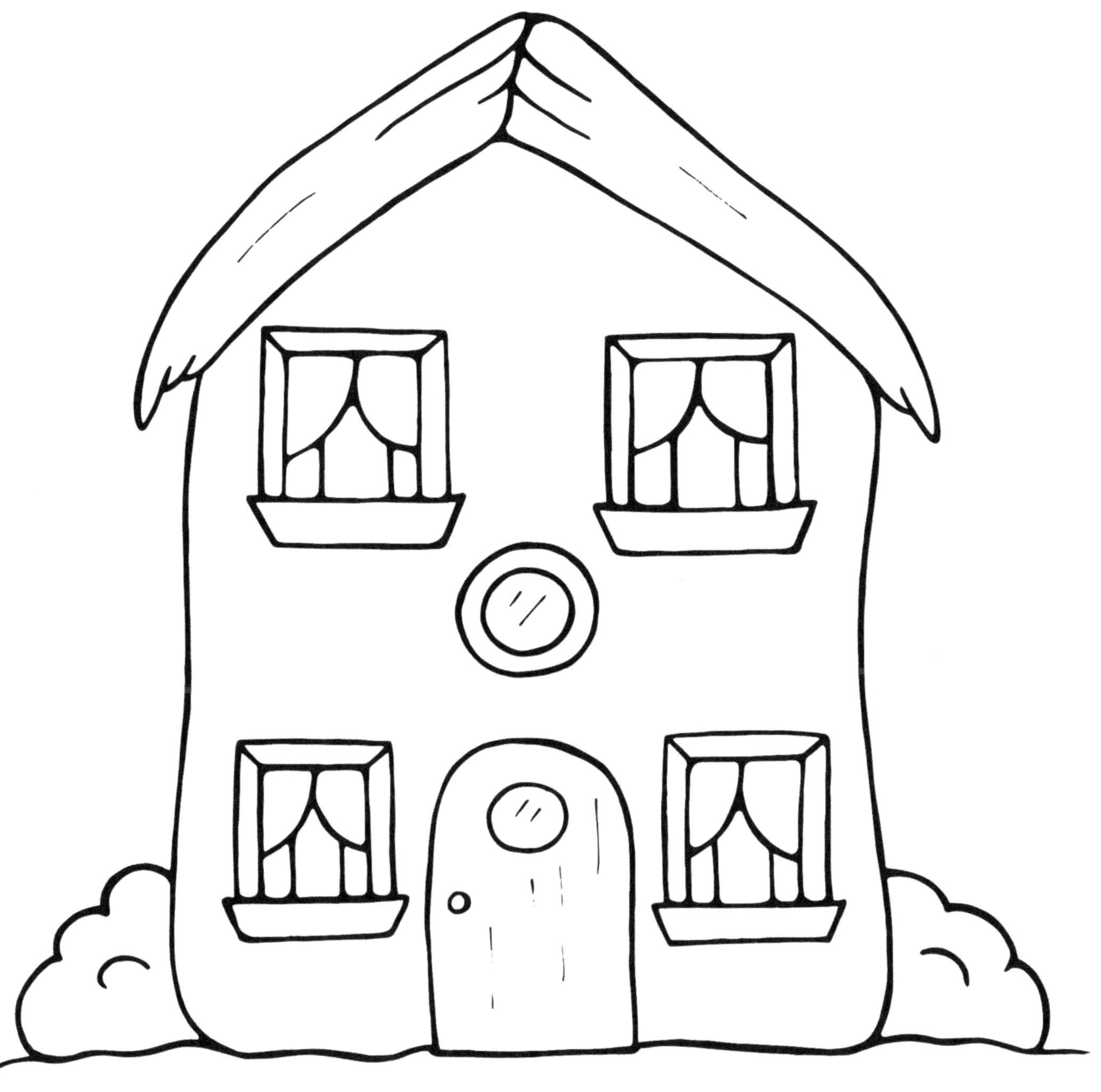

Home ___________ Home

I Love ___________ Cupcakes

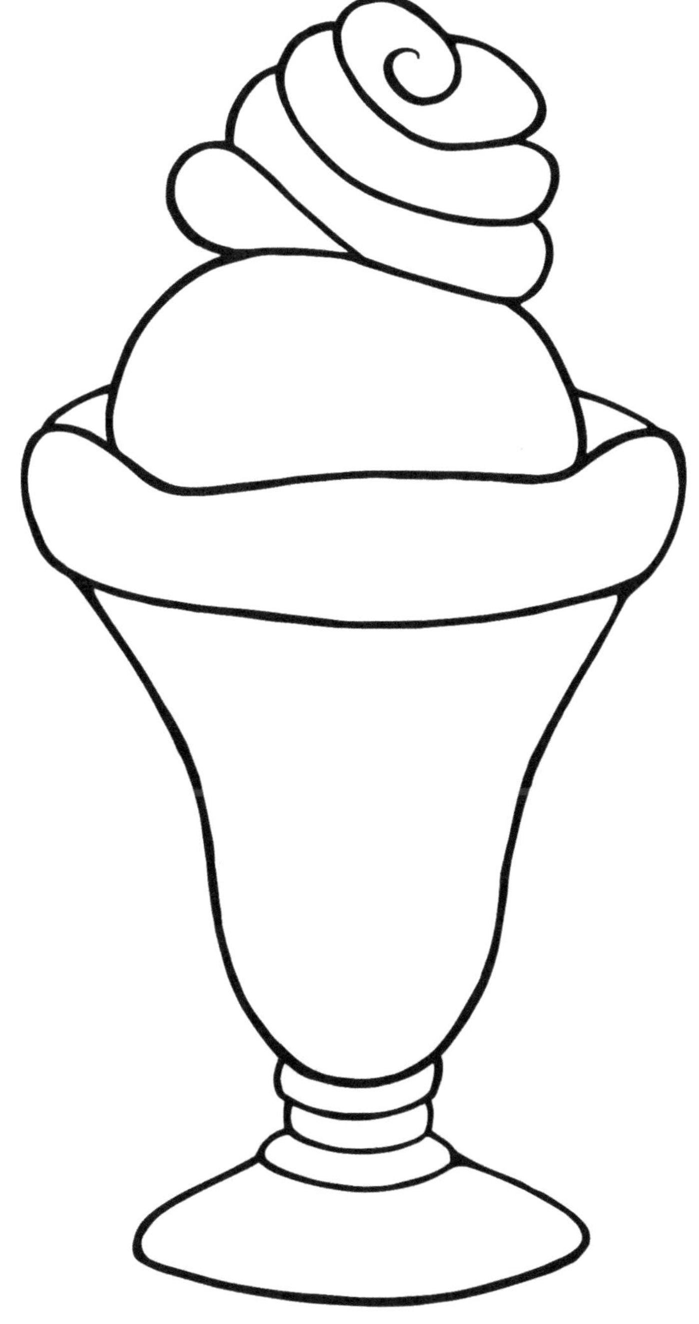

Hot Fudge ____________ Are Delicious

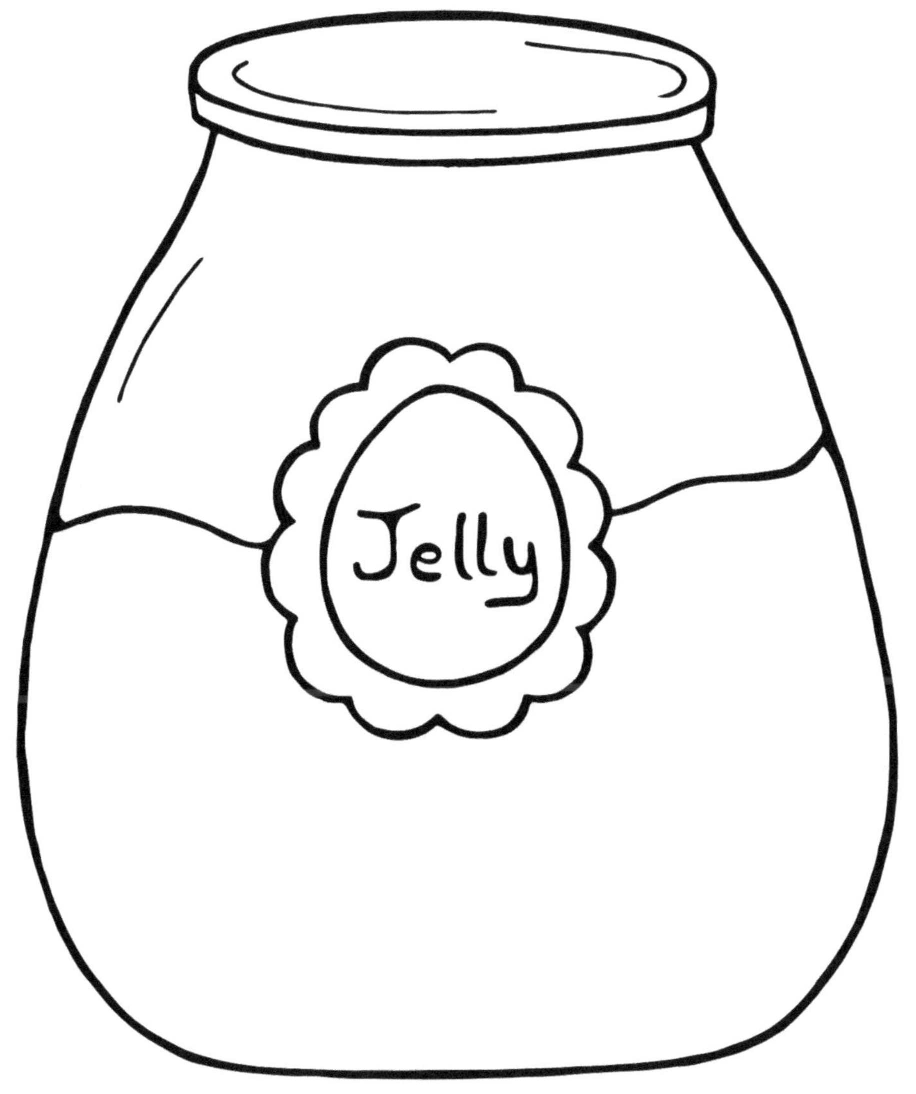

______________ And Jelly

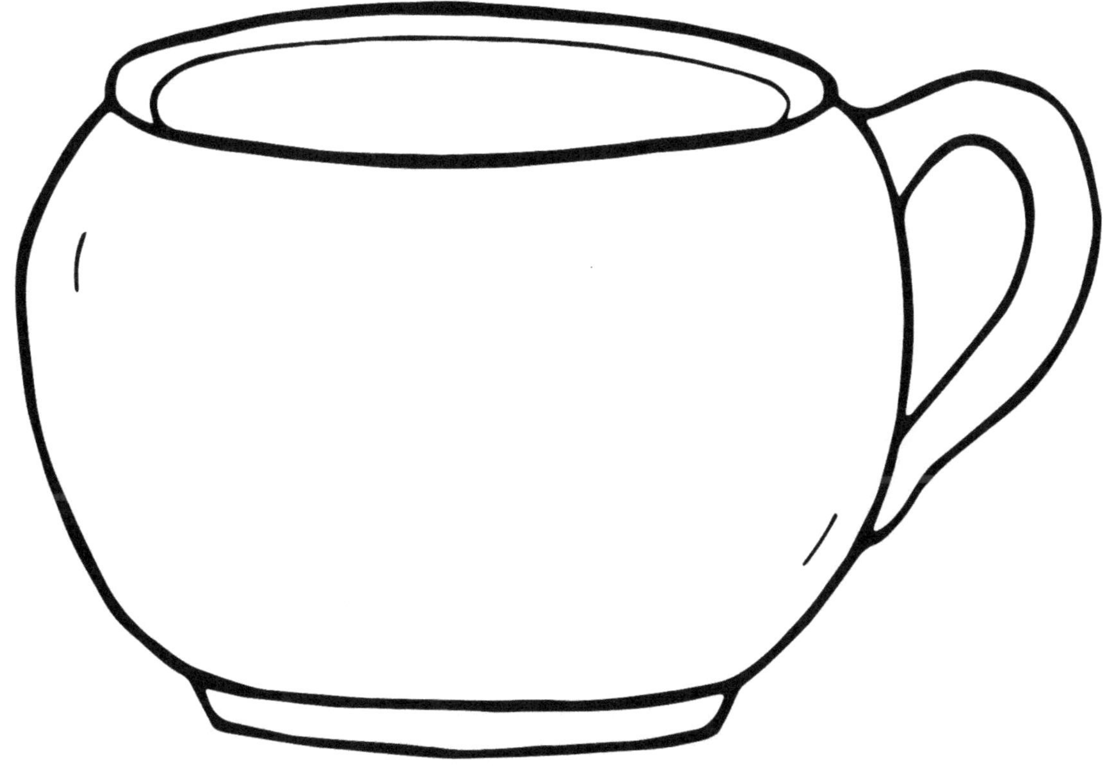

Tea and ___________

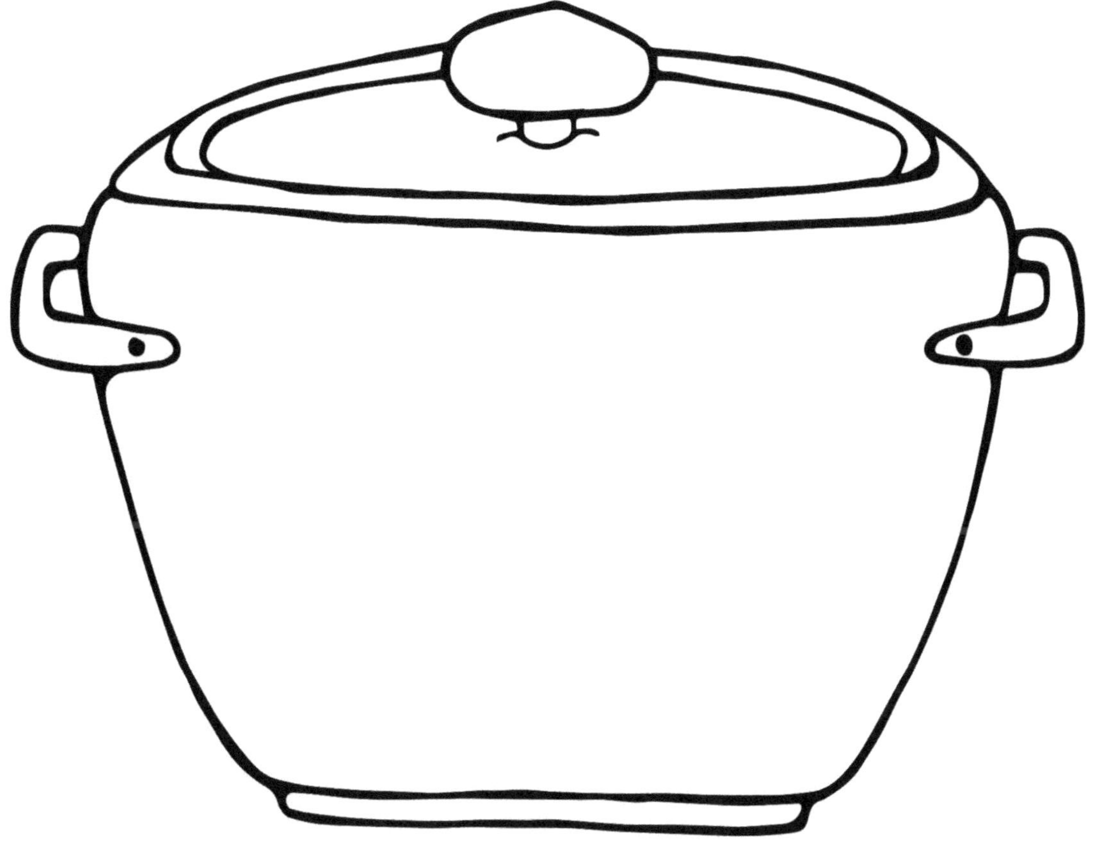

Pots And ___________

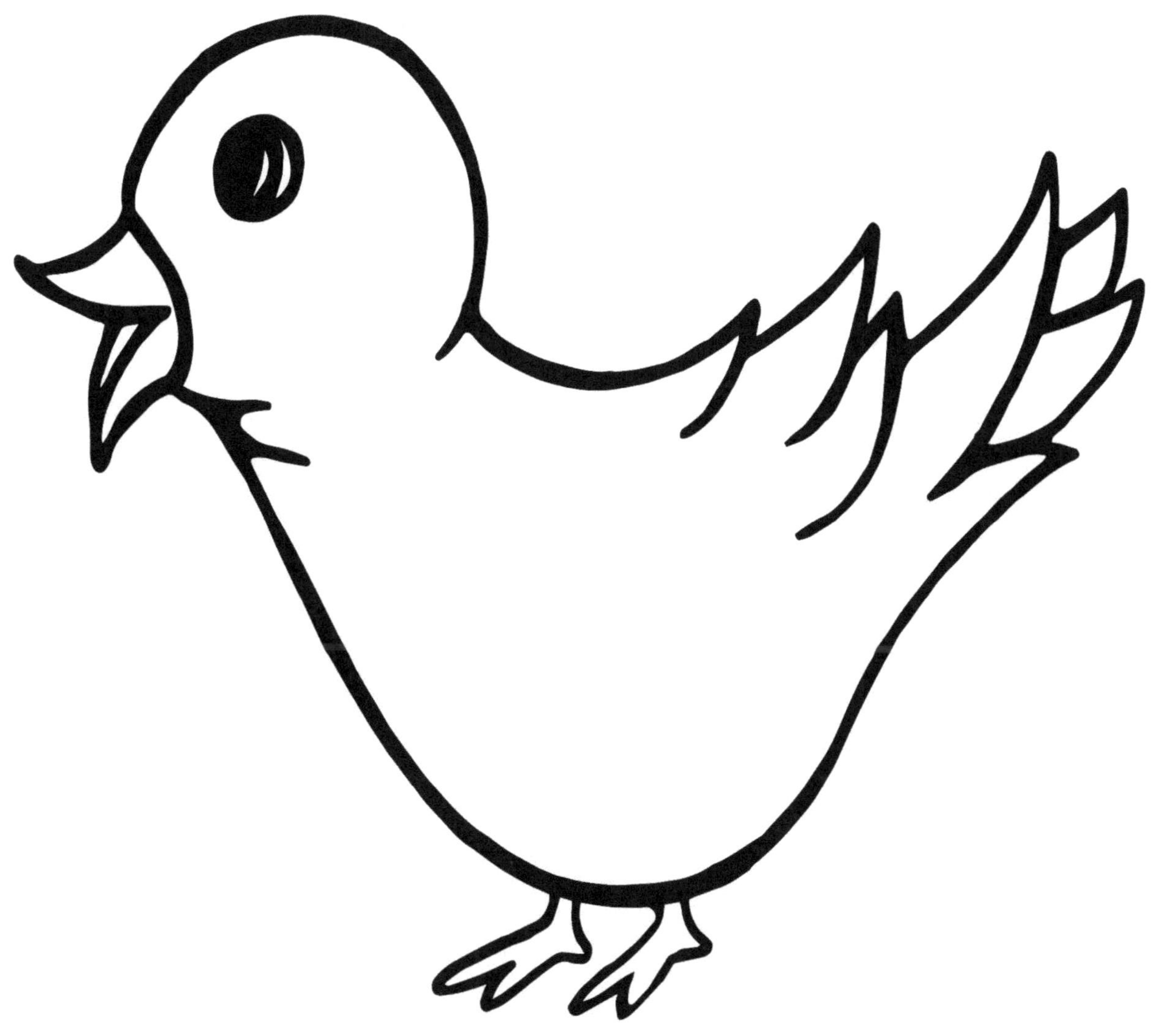

Bluebird On My ____________

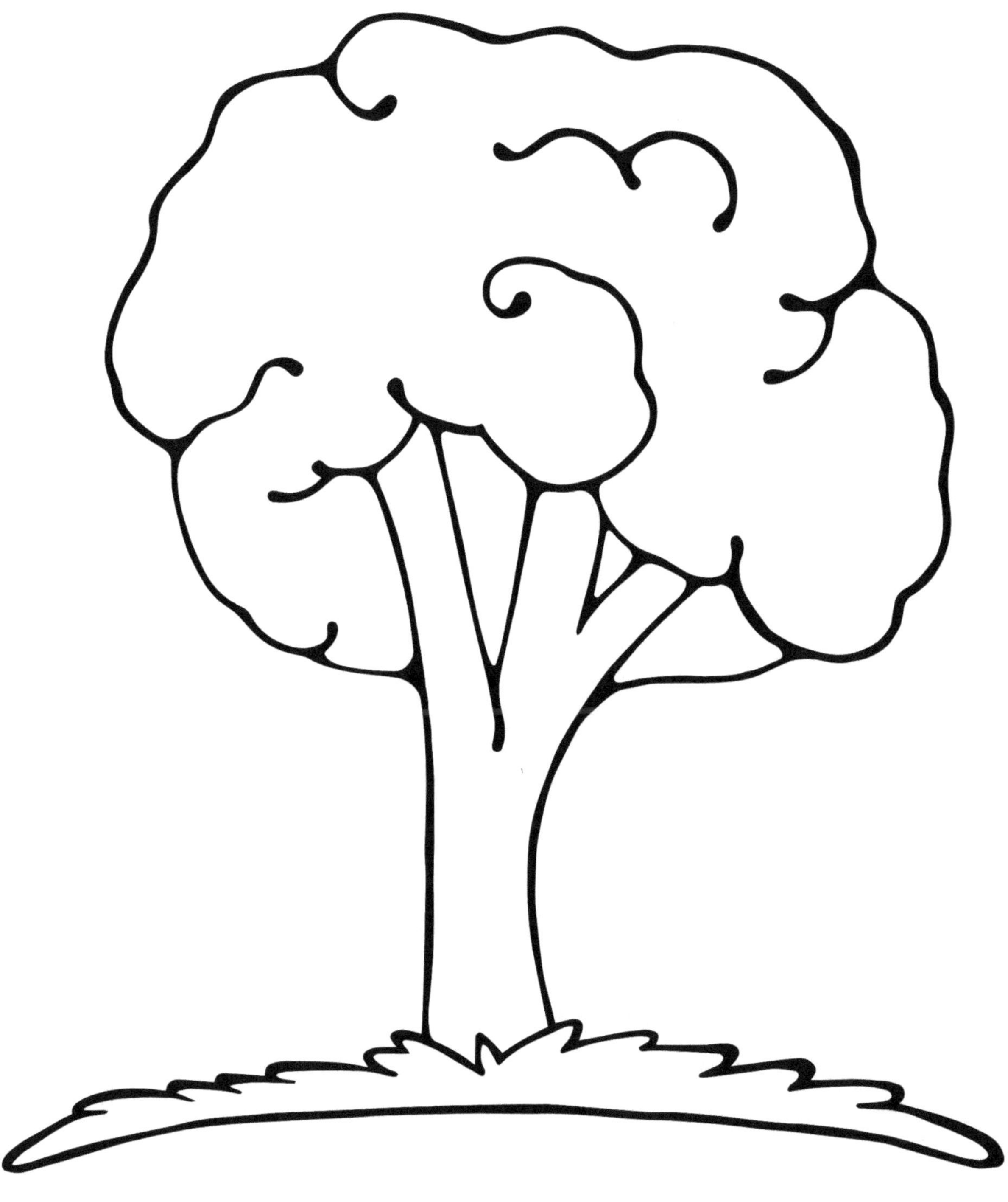

A Tree Grows In ______________

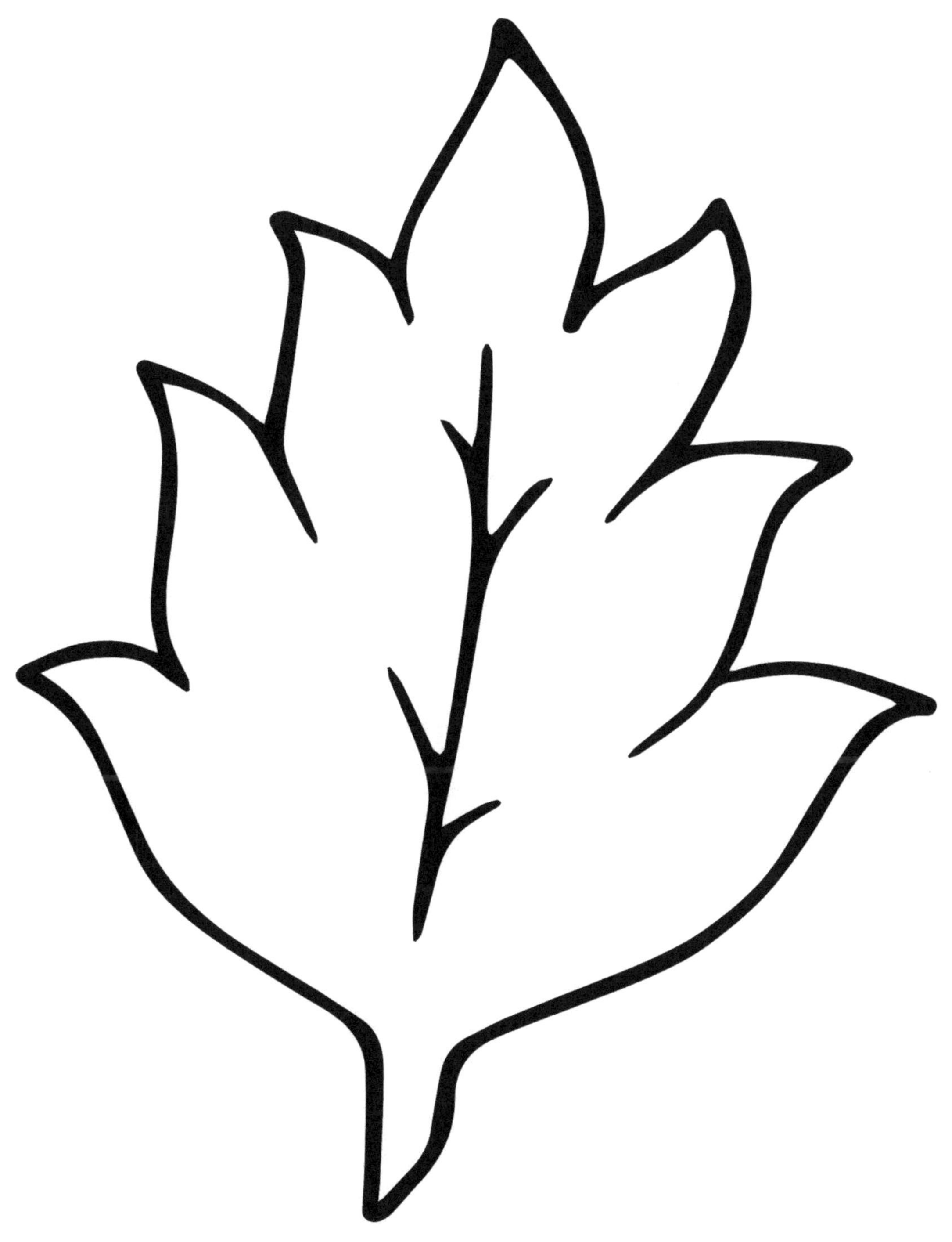

__________ Leaf

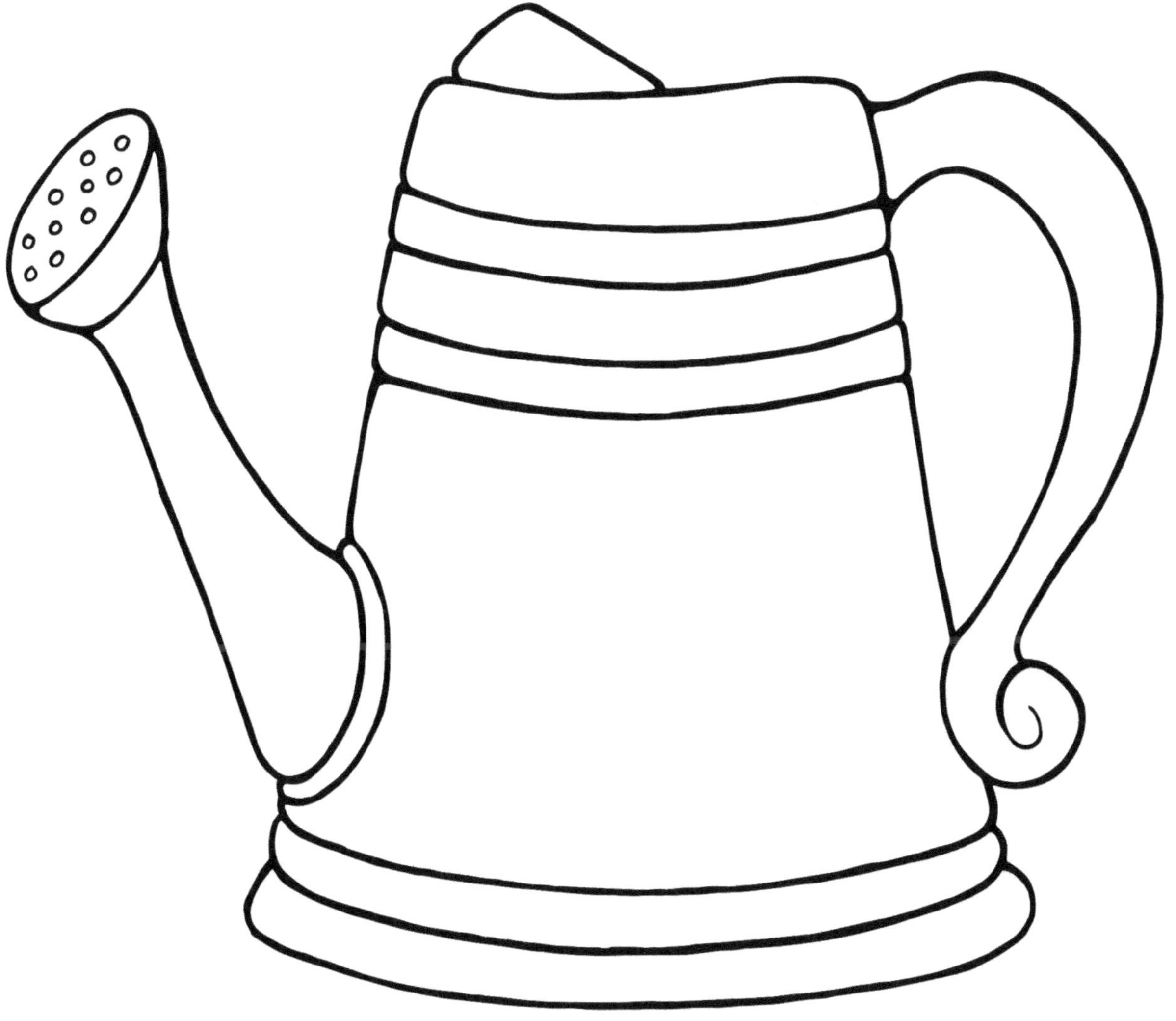

Watering My _____________ Garden

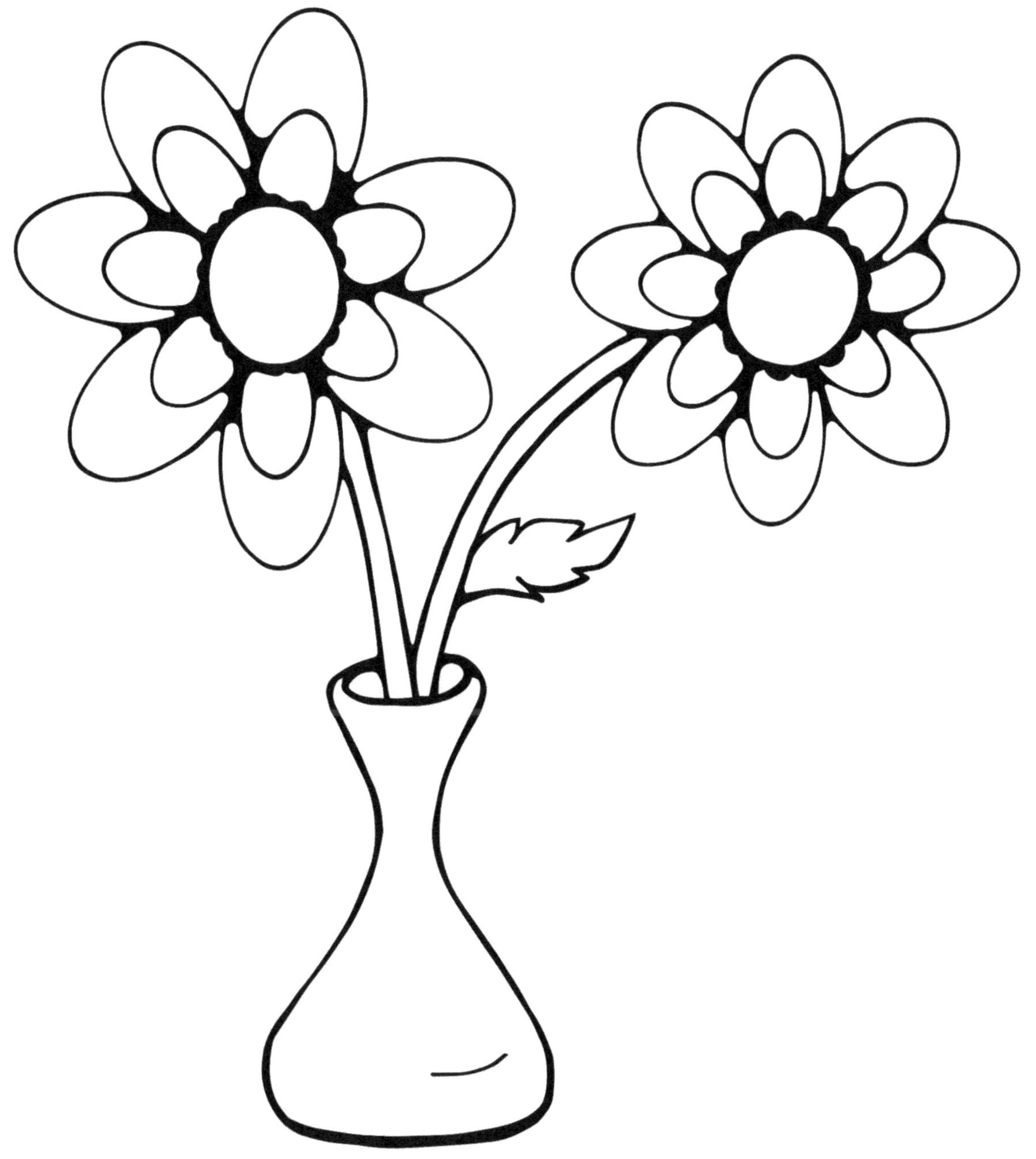

Flowers Make Me ___________

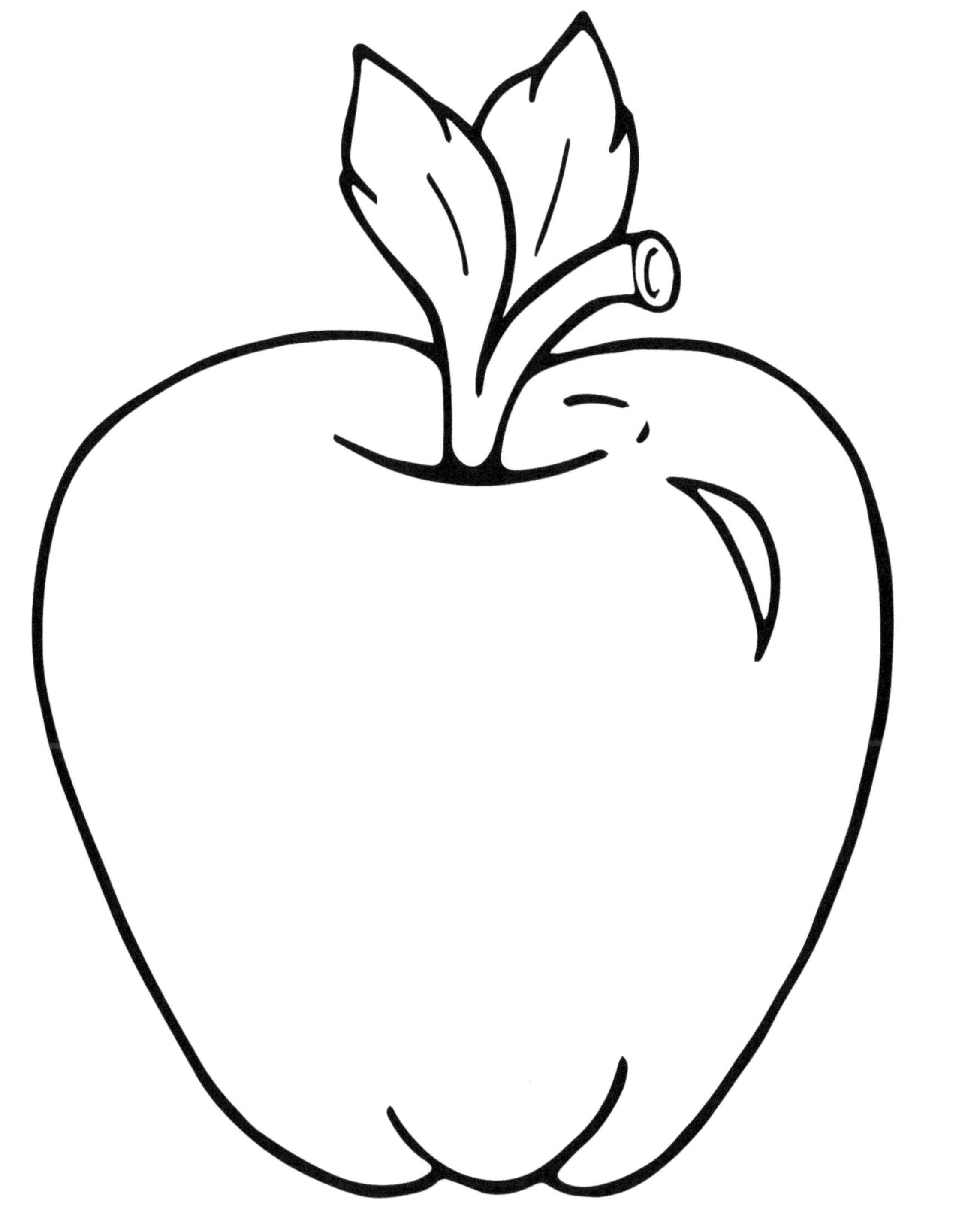

Apple Pie And ___________

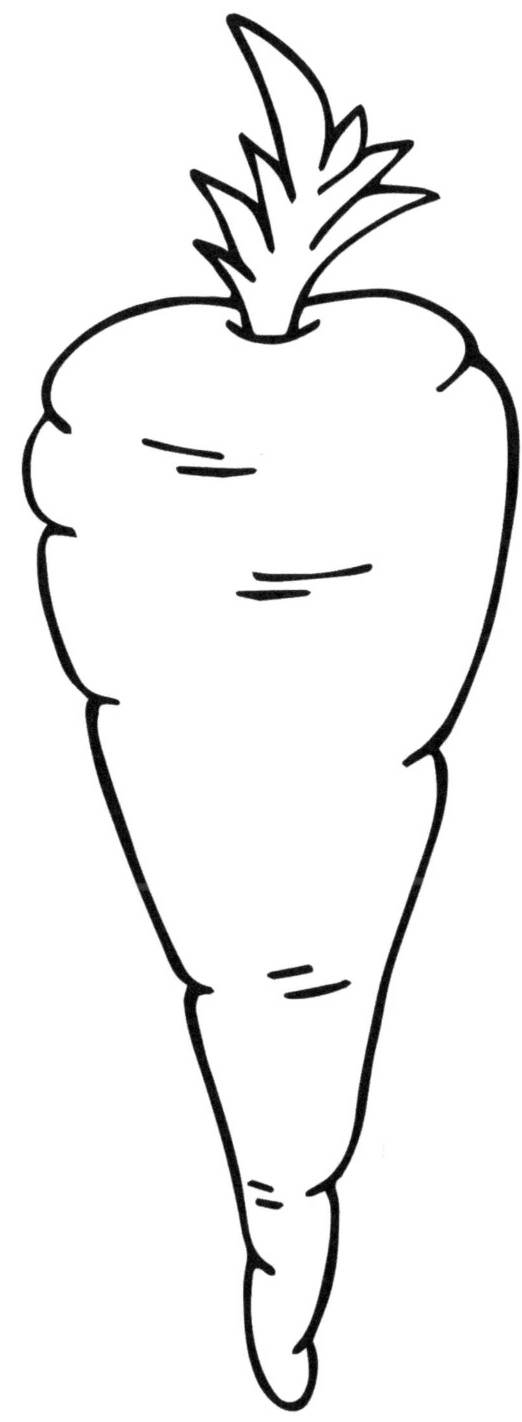

Carrots and ___________

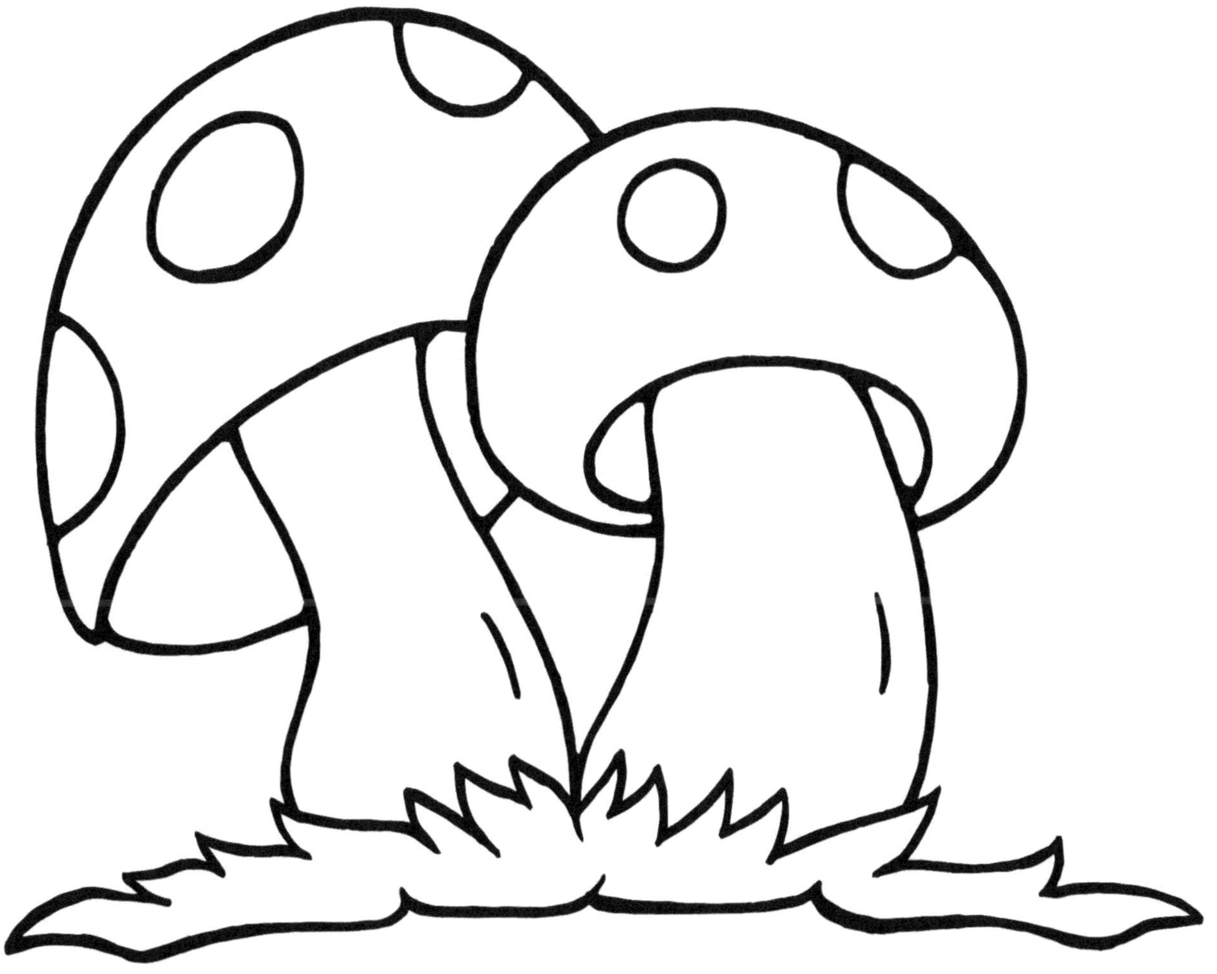

Mushroom ________________

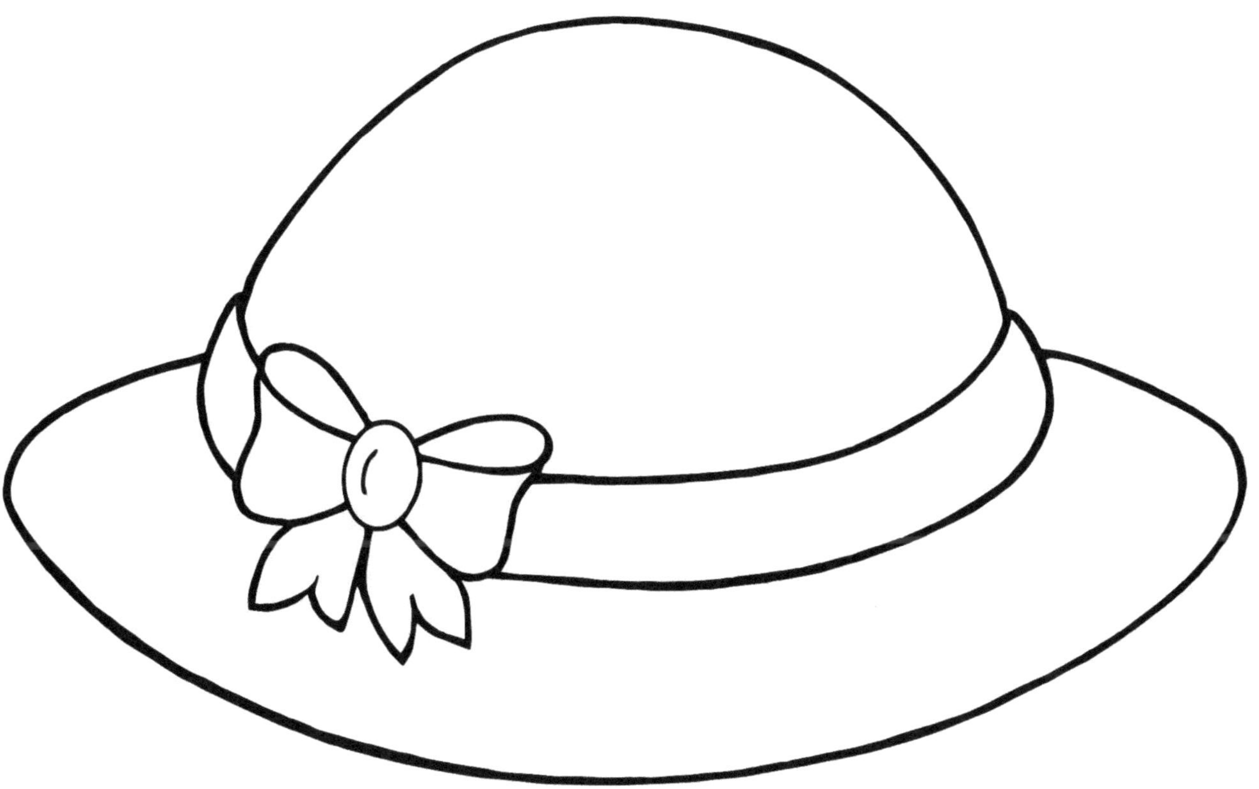

I Love My Pretty ________________ Hat

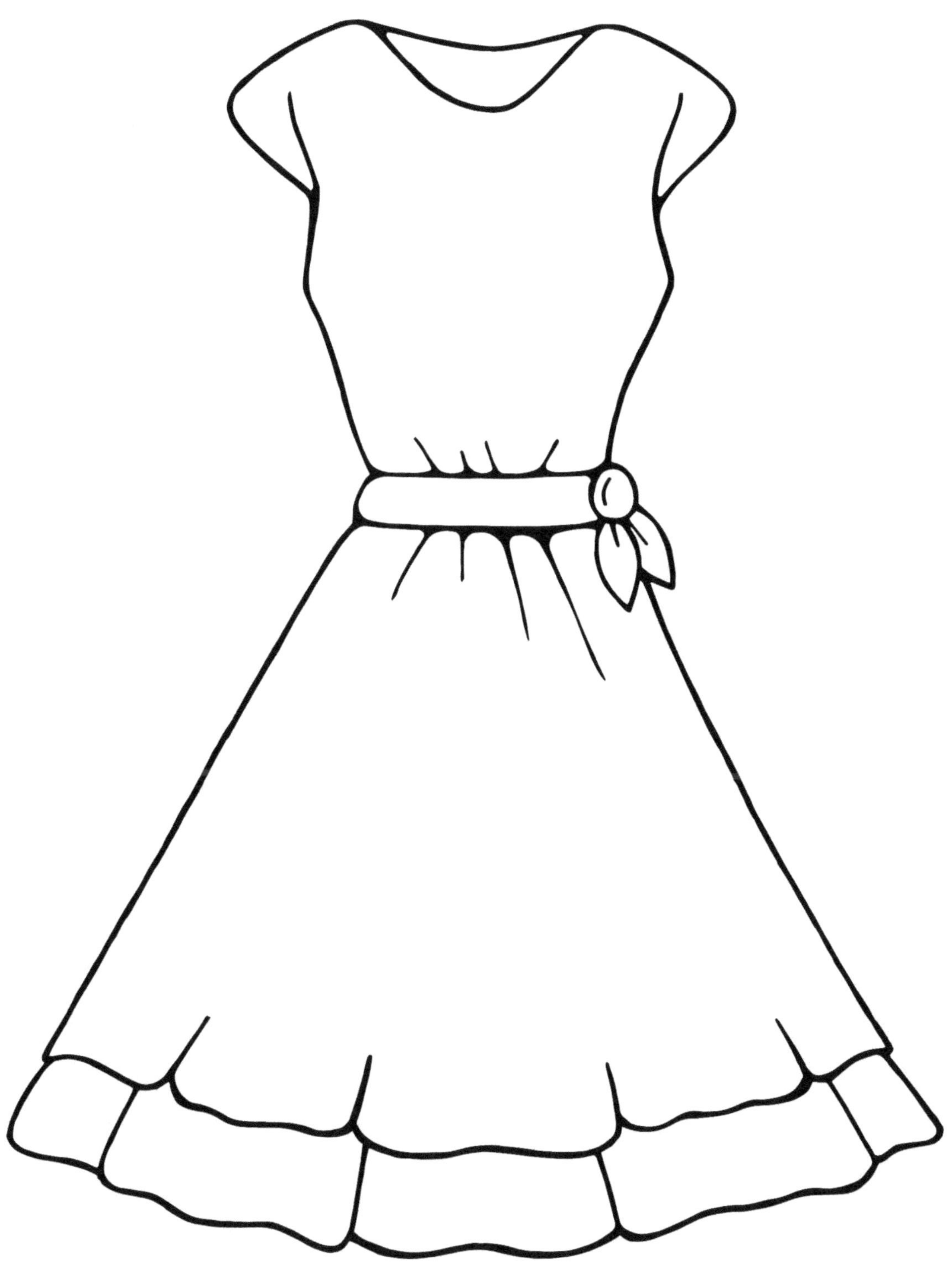

My Favorite ____________ Dress

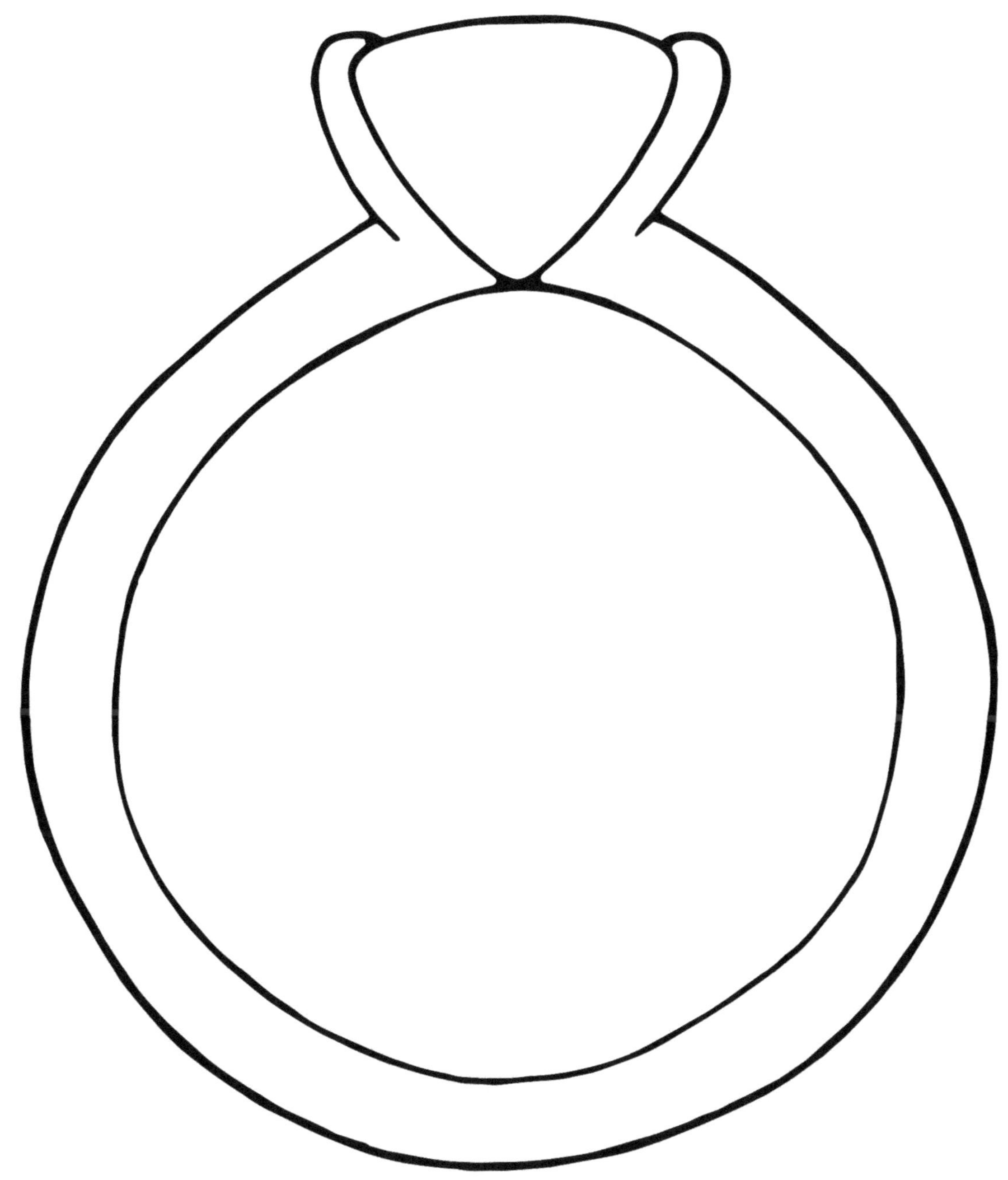

_______________ Ring

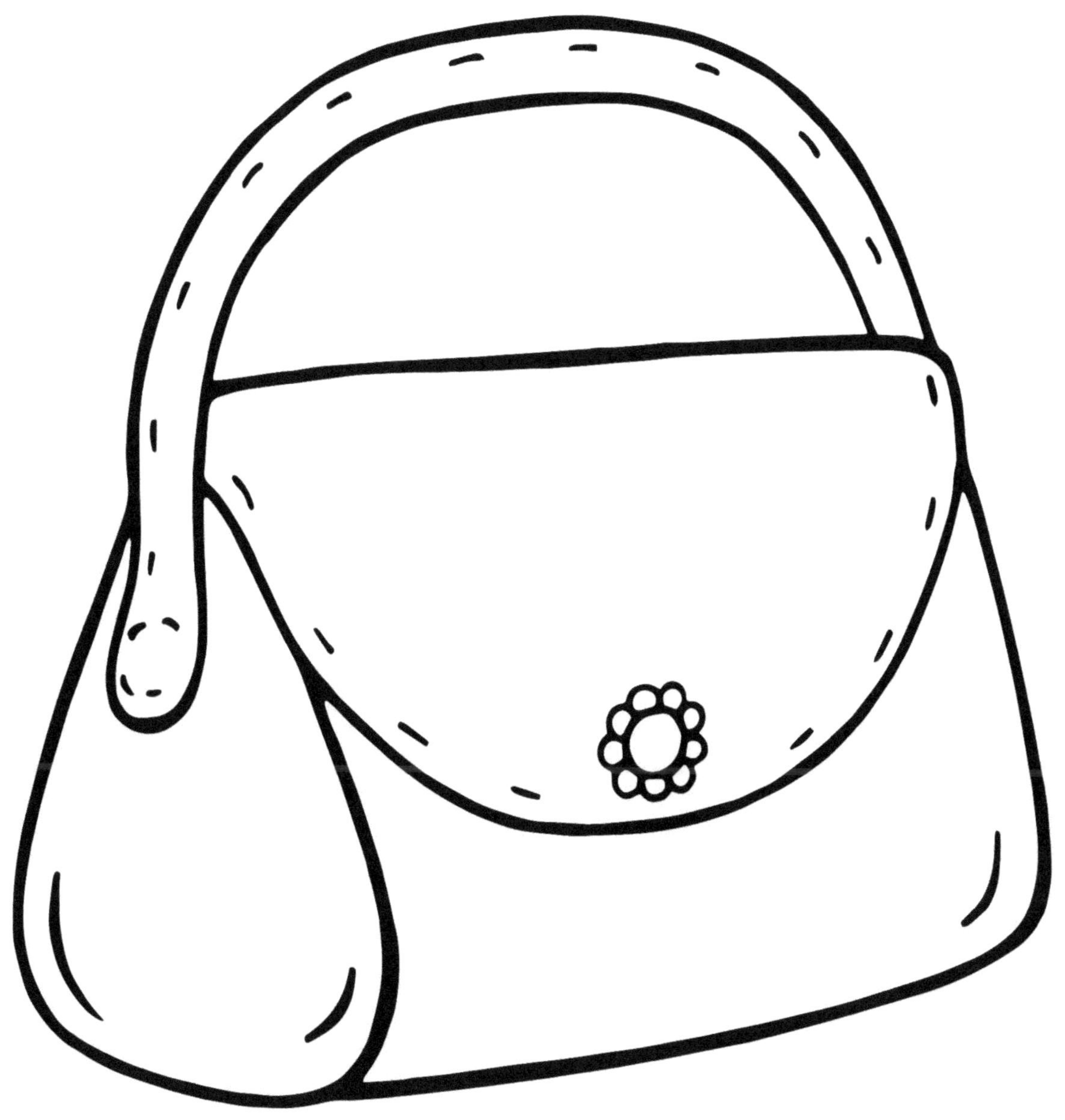

I Have A _________
In My Pocketbook

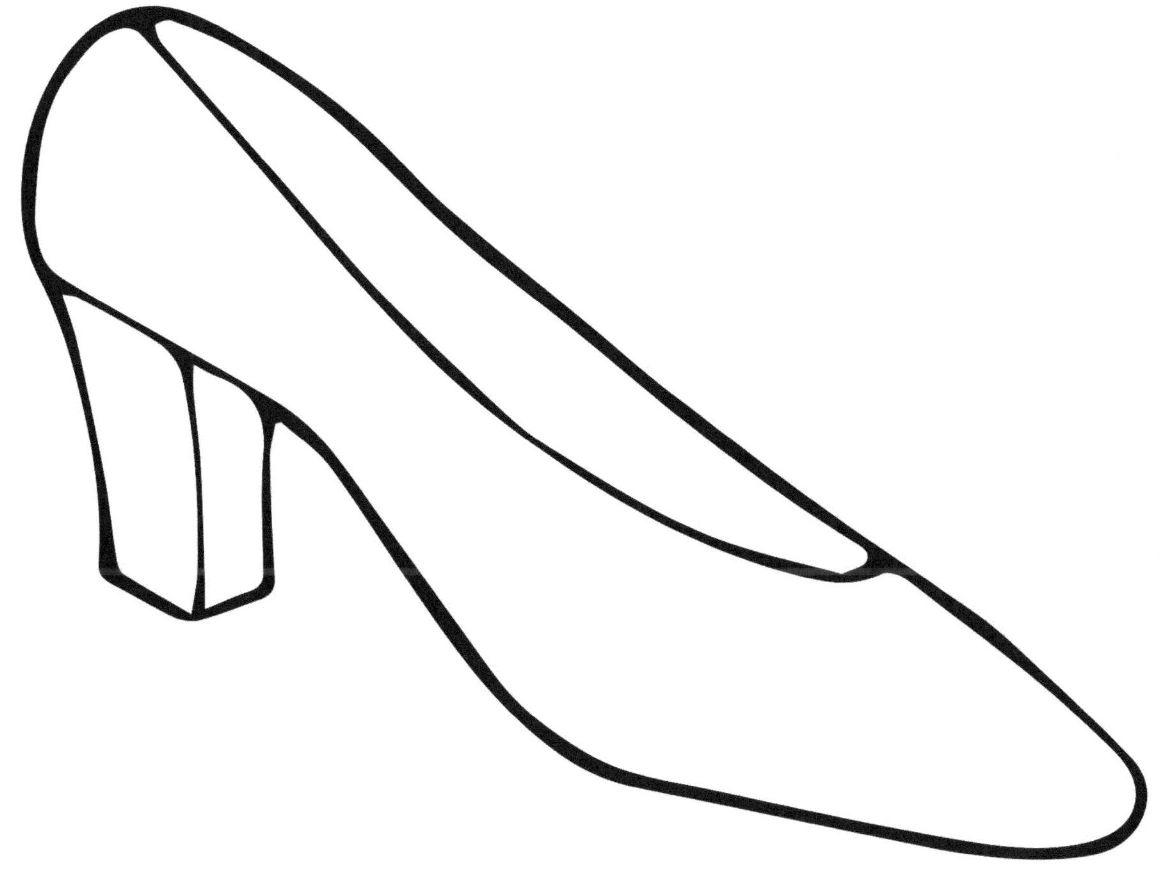

Slip On Your __________ Shoes

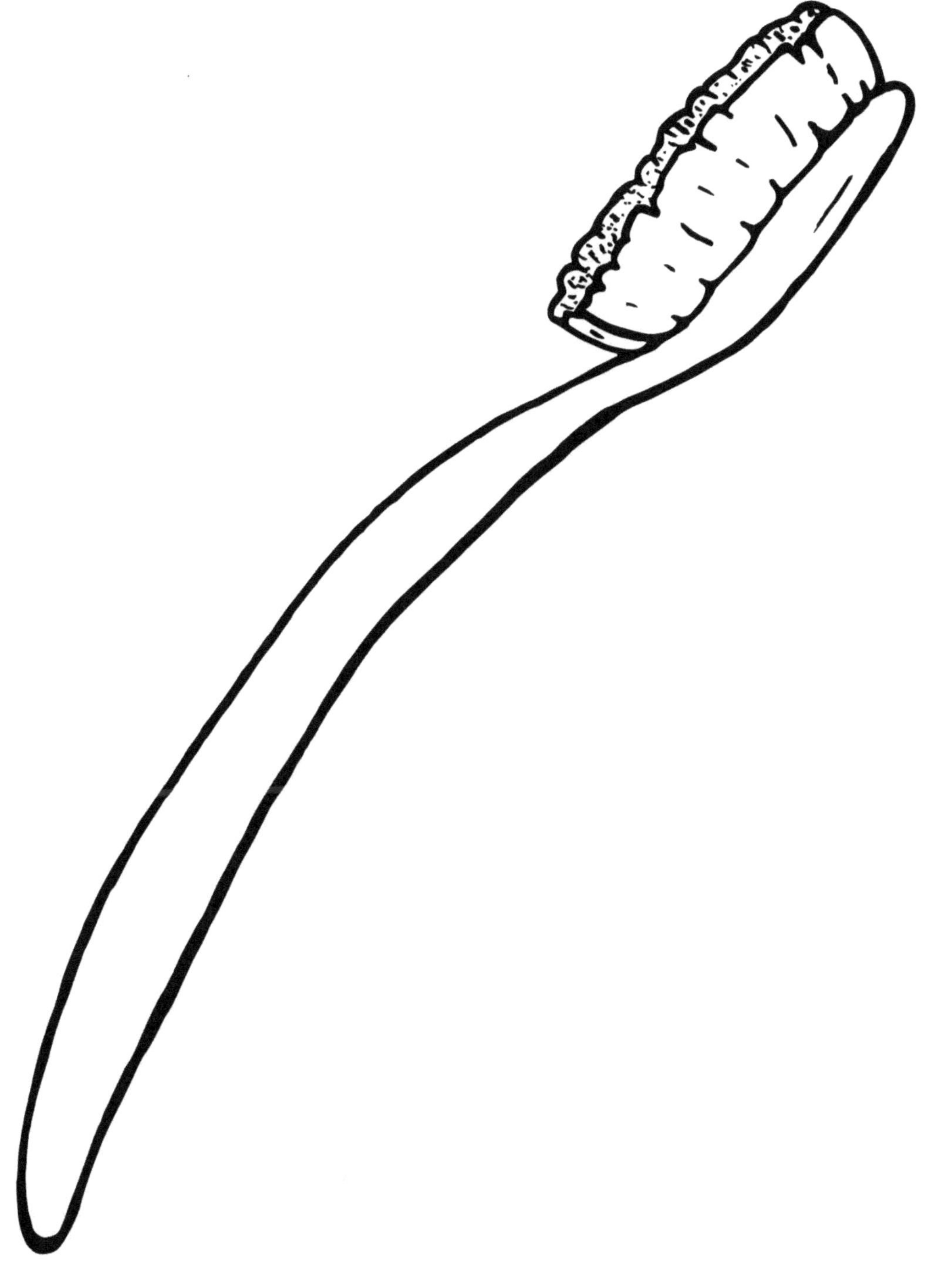

I Brush My Teeth Every ___________

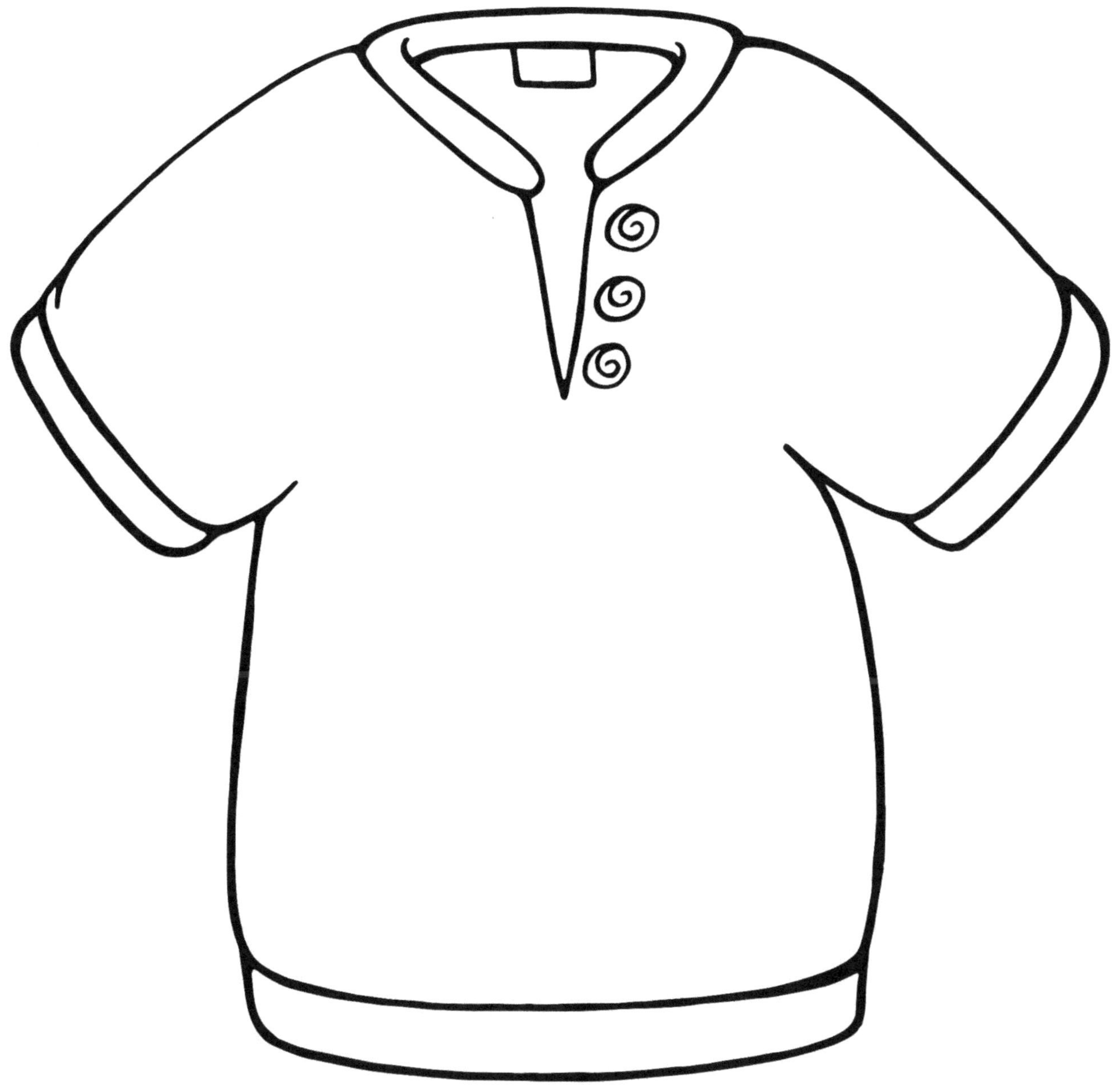

The Shirt Off My ______________

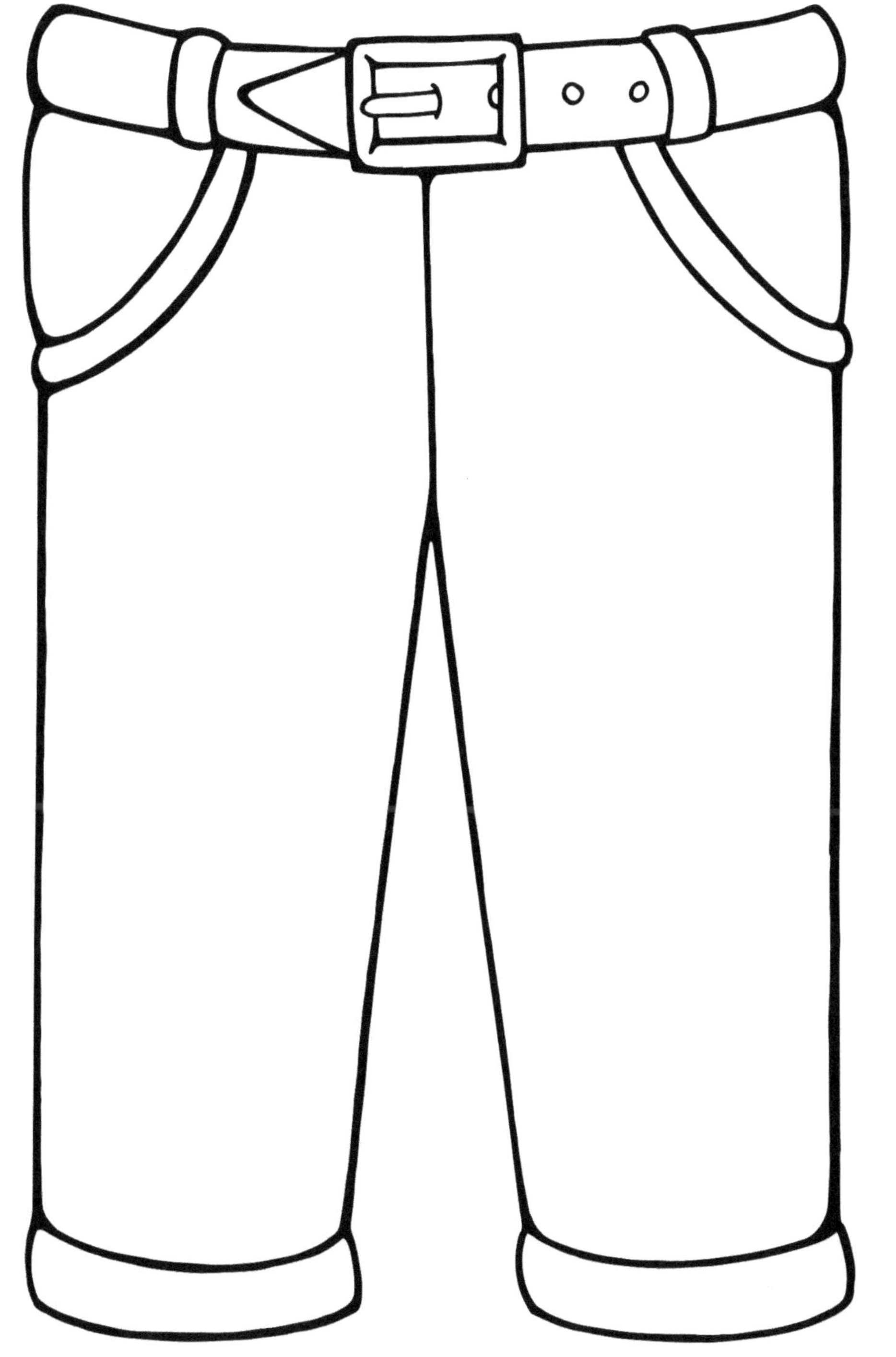

I Wear The Pants In The __________

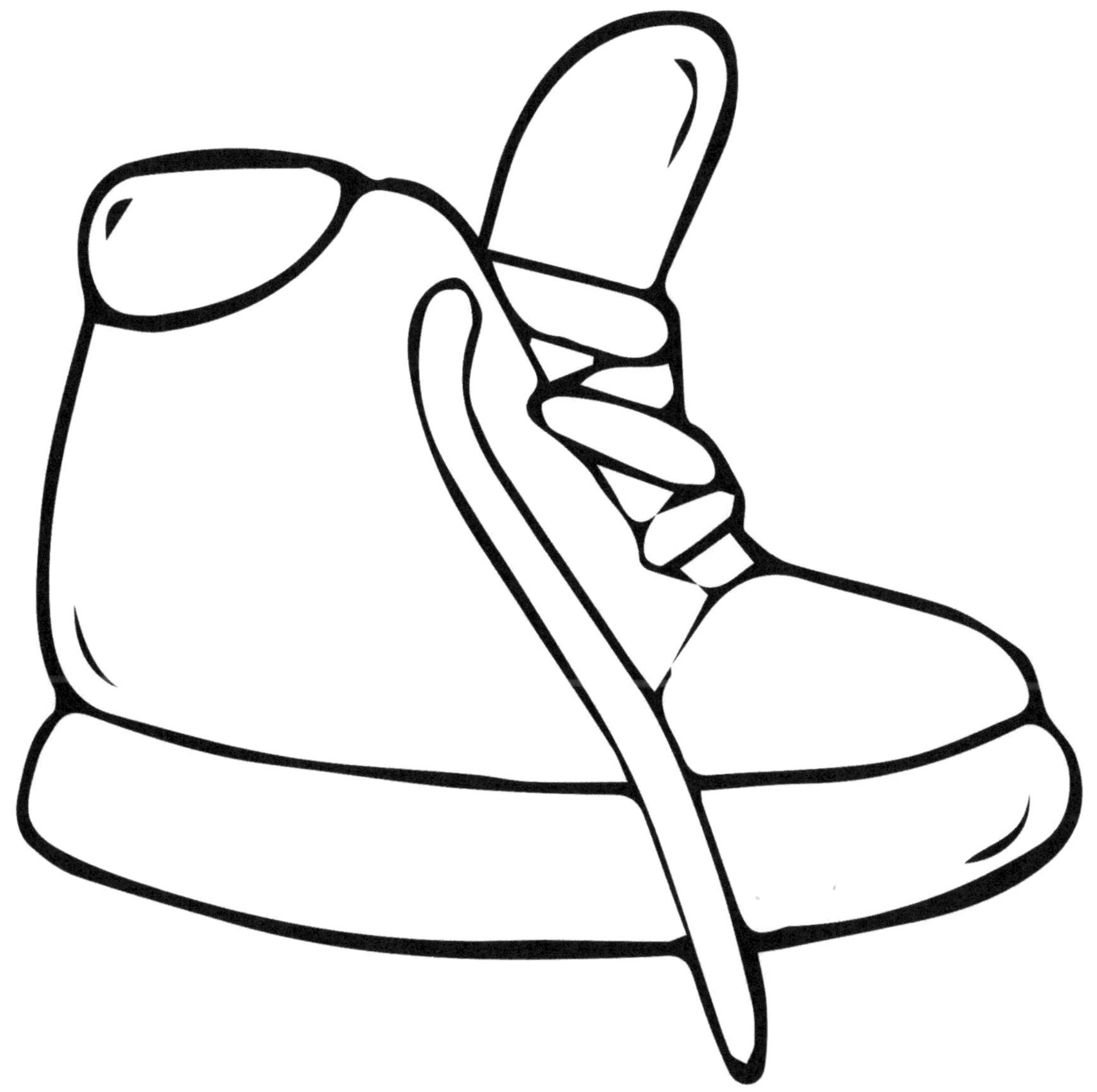

If The Shoe ____________

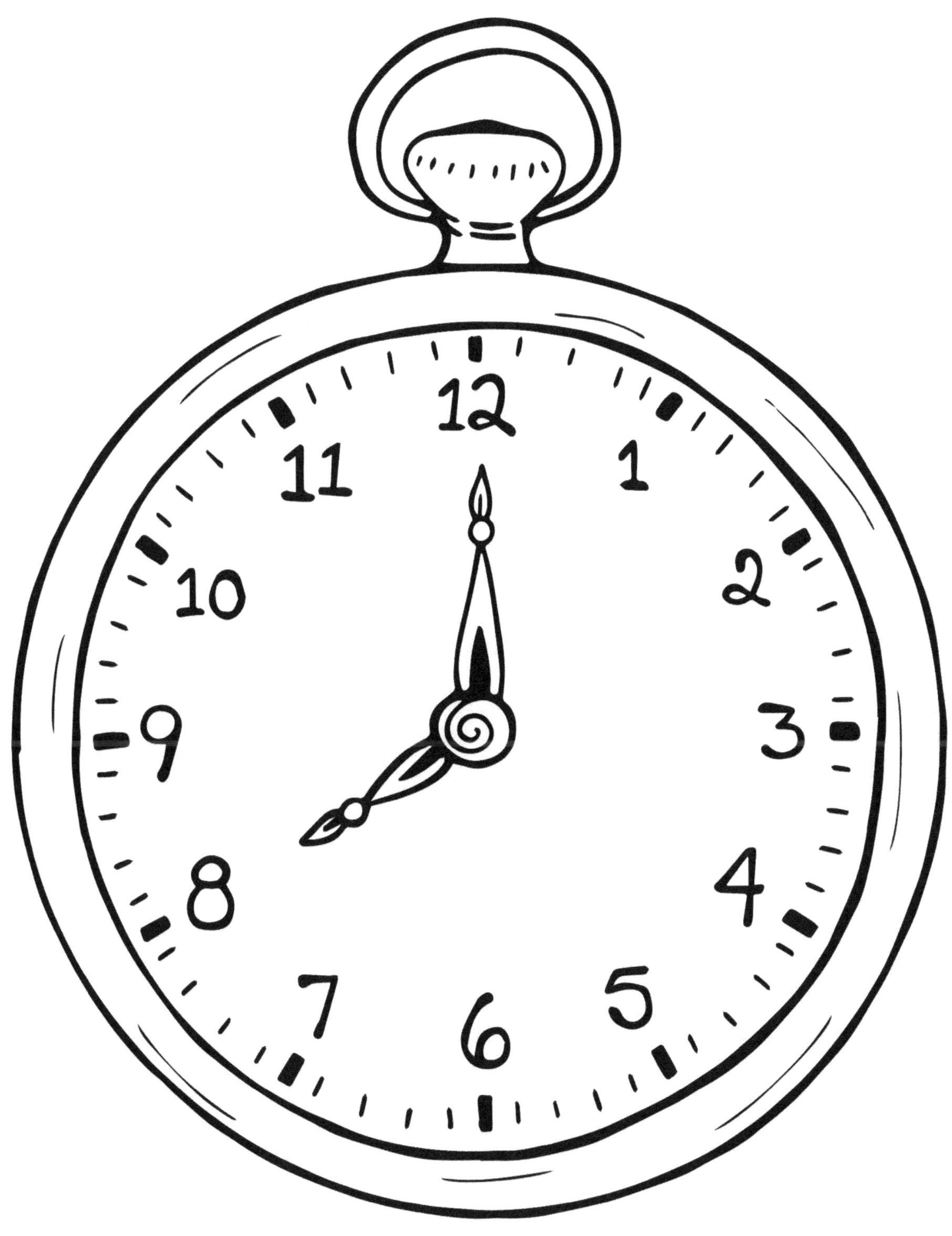

It's Time To Go ______________

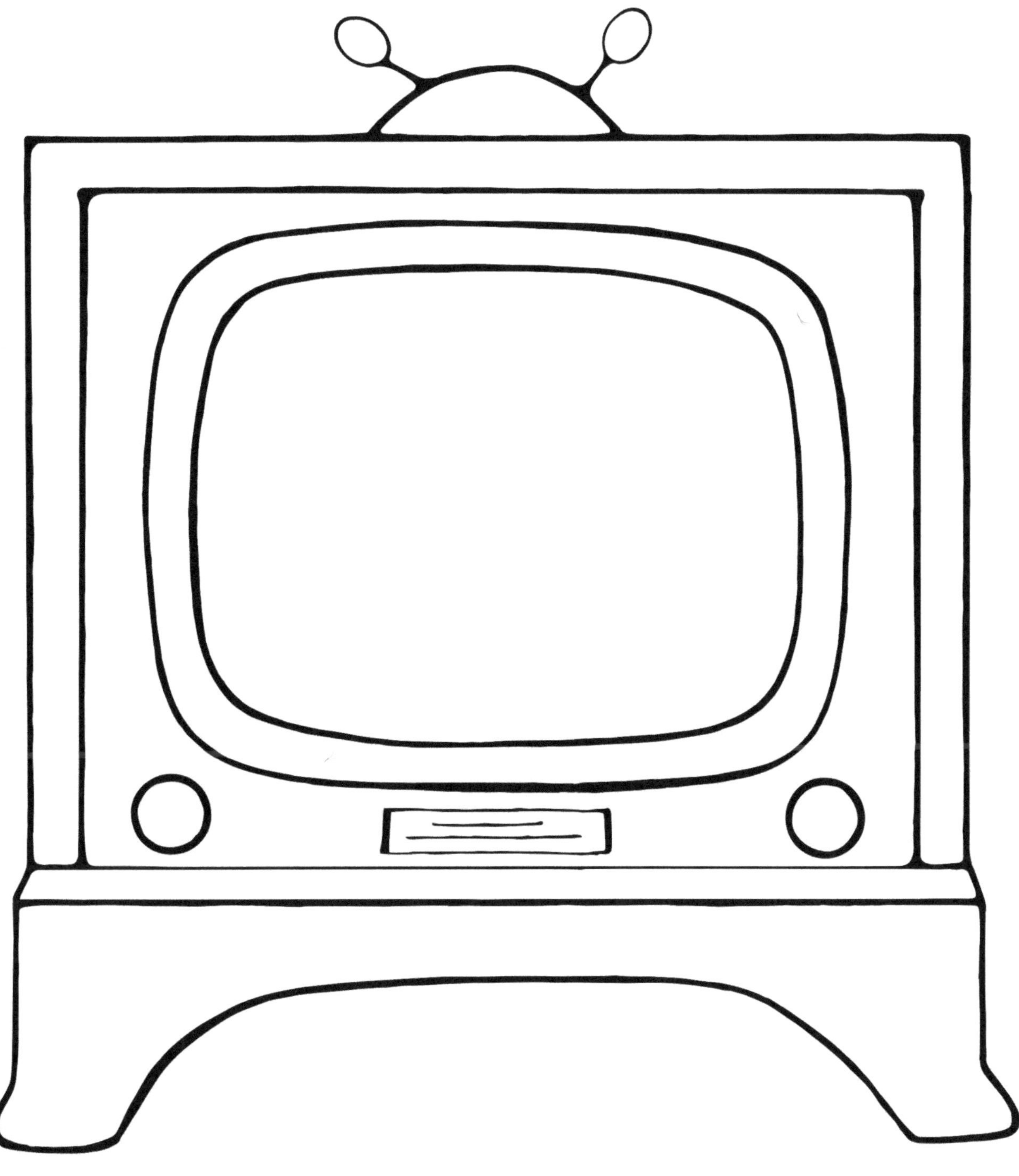

I Watch __________
On The Television

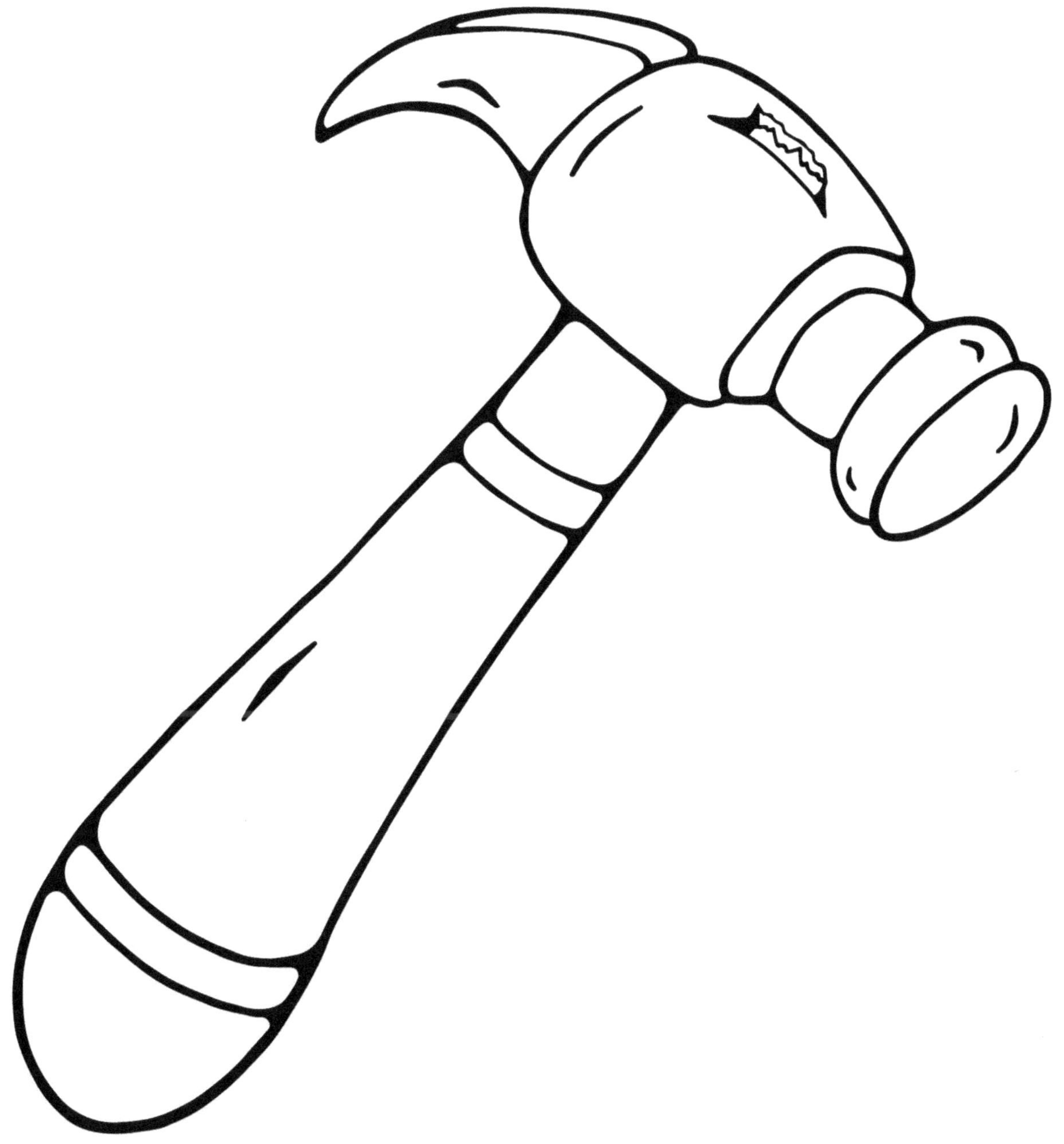

Hammer And ________________

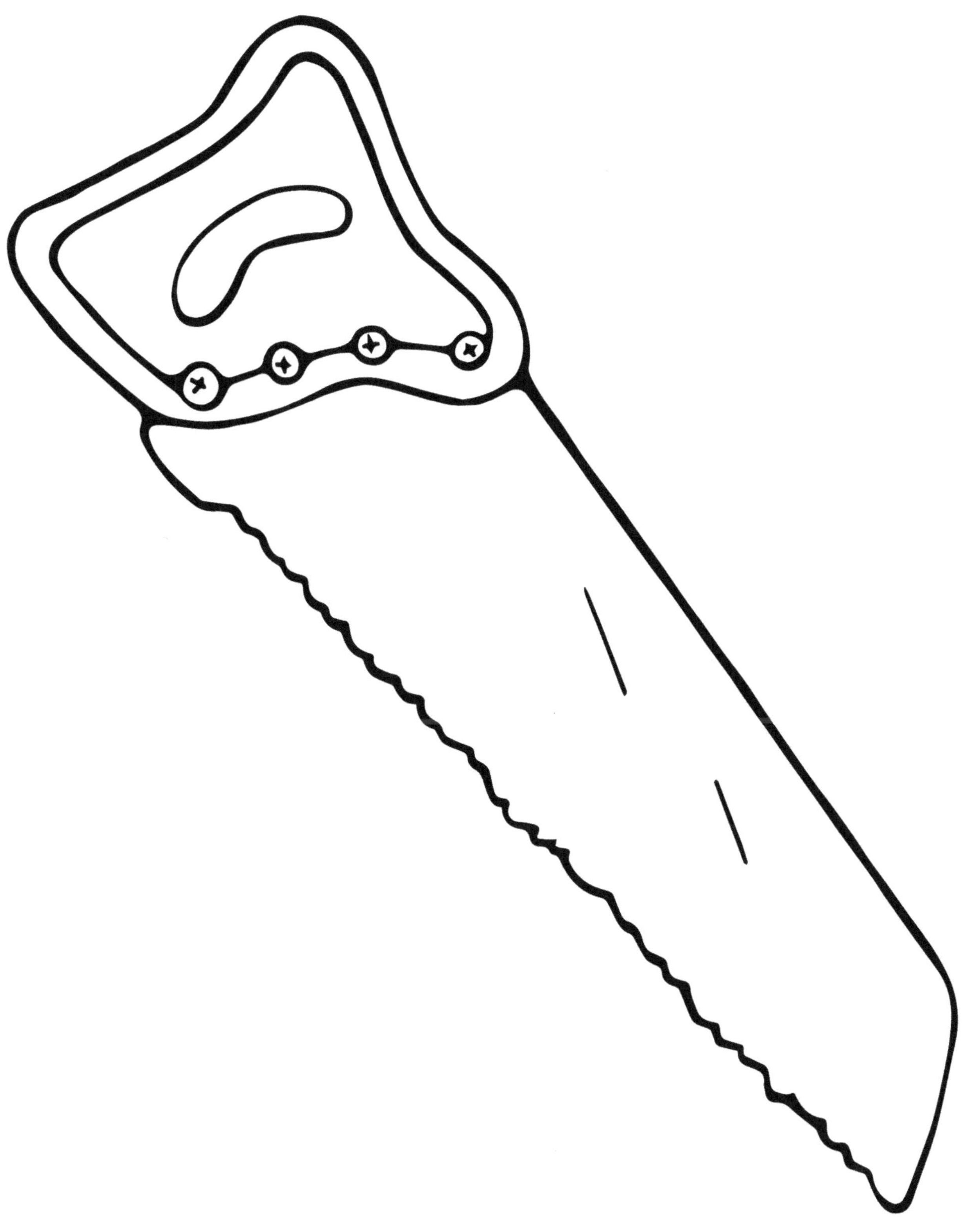

Sawing ____________

www.ingramcontent.com/pod-product-compliance
Lightning Source LLC
LaVergne TN
LVHW081423110826
845149LV00010B/1852